ONCE UPON A DREAM

Pages Of Creativity

Edited By Sarah Waterhouse

First published in Great Britain in 2024 by:

Young Writers
Remus House
Coltsfoot Drive
Peterborough
PE2 9BF
Telephone: 01733 890066
Website: www.youngwriters.co.uk

All Rights Reserved
Book Design by Ashley Janson
© Copyright Contributors 2024
Softback ISBN 978-1-83565-878-9
Printed and bound in the UK by BookPrintingUK
Website: www.bookprintinguk.com
YB0609A

FOREWORD

Welcome Reader, to a world of dreams.

For Young Writers' latest competition, we asked our writers to dig deep into their imagination and create a poem that paints a picture of what they dream of, whether it's a make-believe world full of wonder or their aspirations for the future.

The result is this collection of fantastic poetic verse that covers a whole host of different topics. Let your mind fly away with the fairies to explore the sweet joy of candy lands, join in with a game of fantasy football, or you may even catch a glimpse of a unicorn or another mythical creature. Beware though, because even dreamland has dark corners, so you may turn a page and walk into a nightmare!

Whereas the majority of our writers chose to stick to a free verse style, others gave themselves the challenge of other techniques such as acrostics and rhyming couplets. We also gave the writers the option to compose their ideas in a story, so watch out for those narrative pieces too!

Each piece in this collection shows the writers' dedication and imagination – we truly believe that seeing their work in print gives them a well-deserved boost of pride, and inspires them to keep writing, so we hope to see more of their work in the future!

CONTENTS

Independent Entrants

Leon Adams (11)	1
Grace Green (11)	2
Summer Gaylard (8)	7
Harry Gu (9)	8
Emilia Parasyri (12)	11
Isaac Jones (10)	12
Zaynab Nadat (5)	15
Ruby Gibbons (10)	16
Muaz Abdullah (11)	20
Cynthia Guo (12)	23
Harleigh Trask (10)	24
Katarina Dorian (11)	27
Jessica Taylor (8)	28
Yvetta Dixon (12)	30
Zlata Livtchak (9)	32
Ethan Nason (7)	34
Mya Das (11)	36
Forqan Omar (11)	38
Elise Real-Slavicky (7)	40
Tanvi Kuncham (10)	42
Sarah Dadusc-Sade (11)	44
Tabitha Wilson (10)	46
Addyson Bishop (12)	48
Elizabeth Osborne (11)	50
Lucas Brand (10)	52
Ted Kander (10)	54
Penelope Gilbert (11)	56
Mahdiyyah Ahmed (10)	58
Ayati Pal (11)	60
Mehreen Azim (12)	62
Dhruv Maheshwari (11)	64
Amaan Mughal (11)	66
Emma Nicholas (12)	68
Effie Ellis (10)	70
Elise Thomas (8)	72
Isla Massie (11)	74
Lily Cryer-Richard	75
Fatima Nabeeha (12)	76
Tofunmi Sowanola (11)	77
Kevin Xu (11)	78
Jason Medina (8)	80
Lyra Thomas (7)	82
Jessica Malarini Nirmalan (10)	84
Gareth Wong (9)	85
Mia Istakov (8)	86
Charlotte Dawes (9)	88
Hamish Coles (8)	90
Khadijah Arfan Ahmed (11)	91
Delilah Morrison (9)	92
Mia Ellerington (10)	93
Kairos Sunuwar (10)	94
Alfie Inkster (11)	95
Abigail Living (9)	96
Adeeba Farah (13)	98
Benyamin Mustafa (10)	100
Francesca Lloyd (11)	101
Aria Gaberria (9)	102
Aaliyah Shakoor (10)	103
Myles Joseph (11)	104
Estelle Sutton (9)	106
Ziyang William Li (9)	107
Etta Jordan (9)	108
Adele Bagdonas (11)	109
Meera Jassal (9)	110
Isabelle Gower (8)	111
Catherine Li (7)	112
Penelope Hughes (10)	113
Alistair Butterworth (9)	114
Jessica Lee (10)	115

Summer Byrne-Williams (8)	116
Hafsa Shafiq (10)	117
Dylan Sessions (8)	118
Henry Start (9)	119
Violet King (8)	120
Emma Cooper (10)	121
Alick Patton (11)	122
Diana Strepka (9)	123
Meth Asher (9)	124
Lilly Tyler (10)	125
Hope Miles (9)	126
Laurie Roth (9)	127
Christina Lucille Young (4)	128
Amarachi Obeta (10)	129
Carter Davis (7)	130
Nia Vinod (8)	131
Shanaya Koul (11)	132
Sophia Morath (9)	133
India Patel (10)	134
Onyinye Onwuokwu (6)	135
Erin Murray (8)	136
Kanchan Baishkiyar (11)	137
Natalia Kluk (7)	138
Hannah Morgan (12)	139
Florence Barlow (8)	140
Dayna Speker (10)	141
Sophia Magson (10)	142
Oishika Das (9)	143
Mellisa Afram (11)	144
Sabiha Qasimi (9)	145
Molly Matthews (10)	146
Tilly Chapman (8)	147
Amandeep Bhakar (11)	148
Grace Modesto (8)	149
Chloe Wilkinson (11)	150
Imogen Sims (10)	151
Chloe Clements-Partridge (7)	152
Amyra Qoudos (7)	153
Ellen James (8)	154
Frank Crowther (10)	155
Eleanor Powlesland (9)	156
Tess Crockford (9)	157
George Hill (9)	158
Teja Vasikauskaite (11)	159
Anniyah Samoy-Flores (9)	160
Jessica Woods (9)	161
Evan Phillips (8)	162
Oliver Ruminas (7)	163
Sophie Yarranton (8)	164
Sophie Grace Kennedy (10)	165
Becky Marshall (9)	166
Kiana Gour (10)	167
Rae Denton (6)	168
Rose Field (7)	169
Aaisha Munshi (10)	170
Thomas Living (11)	171
Nico Kitson (7)	172
Còiseam Young (8)	173

THE CREATIVE WRITING

I Live In A Castle

I live in a castle of 17,000 places each and individually unique. It is a cluster of imaginations. It is anything you want it to be. It is made of metal, paper, and wood. It is very strong, like the strongest substance on Earth.
It has aeroplanes that can transform into any flying vehicle that has not been invented yet, or never will be. The castle is filled with extraordinary sights and unimaginable places. In this little world, there is a pen, a mirror, and a chair. It has lights made out of stars and pictures that change colour.
There are places that have trees older than the sun, with blue, white, and grey leaves. The candy tastes like rainbows, and the flowers smell like lavender and vanilla. This world is filled with the beautiful tweets of birds. It is filled with the chirping of ducklings and their soft, smooth, silky feathers, and lilac grass dancing in the wind.
You can think of an object and it will appear, or surf on big wood planks in the ocean of pastel turquoise water. Things are different here with buildings that can change locations of your choice to torches with pink fire that will never run out. Sometimes, I like to play around with the floating bricks or the pencils that can write by themselves, and sometimes I snap out of it and realise how dull the world really is.

Leon Adams (11)

Fairy Tales Aren't What They Seem

Dragon's fire crowds the night,
Not trying to prevent a villager's fright,
A hero is what this village needs,
A hero and their noble steed.

Where would this saviour come from,
Would he be from far and long?
Could this hero be a lord?
Could this hero bring a horde,
Of nobleman to come to their aid,
A group of heroes to save the day?

What is a hero to you?
Could your hero be someone you know,
Could your hero be your bigger bro,
Could it be someone who you look up to,
A celebrity, an uncle or aunt once knew?
For this town, a hero was a knight,
A knight who could show them the light.

The village scouted,
A saviour was doubted,

The dragon laughed,
And had a craft
About what to do next,

Until the villagers left.

They ran to the next-door town,
To find someone to take the dragon down.
The village next door could provide,

At the cost of the village being able to reside,
In the place they were banned from,
The day when the local prom,
Went horribly wrong,
The dragons let loose,
People were banned.
Lives were stolen.
Result - the present situation.

Have you ever done something wrong?
Maybe sing the wrong lyrics to a song?
Just know

Failure is the highway to success

A hero was sought,
And eventually bought,

But not what the village thought.
This hero was no nobleman,

But a noblewoman.

She grabbed some weapons,
Despite her imperfections,
Rushed over to the village,
With no privilege,
Ran into a house,
Prepared and headed south.

"This dragon isn't nice,
So it's time to put things right," she'd say.
"Yer a right fool!" the blacksmith would reply.
"Don't lie!" the village protests,
As the blacksmith got upset,
"Just do it! Before you make me cry!"

She drew her sword,
The dragon roared,
Swing, slash, roar!
The dragon blew its fire,
And advanced higher,
An arrow flew,
Is the dragon due,
For the underworld,

The afterlife,
Has it had enough of this fight?

It hit the dragon,
Acting savage,
It was ravaged,
It hit the eye,
Skimmed the mouth,
For all we know, it's headed south.

A hole in the tail,
Only a little bit of nail,
Missing one eye,
This dragon just got shy,
A part of the mouth,
- This was very with strouth -
A hole in the heart,
Don't do this if you're smart.

She grabbed the dragon's tail,
In the hole, put a nail.
The dragon cried out,
And looked up at the clouds,
It roared,
And went up into the skies,

This must be the end of its life.

Have you ever fought something,
Or someone, in any way? Don't. In a fight,
No one ever wins. A fairy tale, maybe, but
In your fairy tale, it may not work as well.

Keep on dreaming,
And you'll stay gleaming,
Figure out something that works for you,
No matter what you do,
Everyone has their thing.

So, you find yours.

Grace Green (11)

Cosmic Kitsunes

I go to sleep, what a slumber,
I have a dream, what a number,
I see a cave with crystals and vines,
I bet if it were real, there'd be mines.
I'm sided by a Kitsune who's very fond of me,
I think I'll call her Lee.
We enter the cave and, to our astonishment,
We see a golden, furry tuft: dullness abolishment.
Letting my intrusive thoughts take over,
I lean over and touch the golden tuft,
I suddenly feel sick, my body begins to transform,
I turn into something mystical and cosmic,
I feel my new tails, I'm a cosmic Kitsune!
My now relative companion accompanies me.
I'm so shocked, I'm so... confused.
I feel so... alive,
Me and Lee walk outside,
Only to see now a swarm of stars, not a drought outside,
But several other cosmic Kitsunes,
All bounding left and right, through the stars,
But before I know it, I'm awake.

Summer Gaylard (8)

The Battle Of Britain

It was a gloomy morning when,
All at once the alarms all sounded,
And all the aviators rushed to their Spitfires,
For the Luftwaffe were coming.
With a deafening roar, they rose to the sky,
Looking for the bombers to target and enflame.
Agile and nimble were their Spitfires,
Twisting and turning, looking for the Luftwaffe that were coming.

There a voice came over the radio, "They're above us!"
And so, the squadron of twenty climbed up to the fire hell on them,
Up they flew, ready to fire hell on the Luftwaffe,
With all they had.
Their duty, their honour,
To defend the country they knew,
Shun their lives,
Shun their children and their wives,
Their duty to do and die.

Bomber to the right of them,
Bomber to the left of them,
Bomber in front of them,

Fired shot and shell,
But the warbirds dodged and weaved,
Valiantly cut through their lines,
Occasionally firing a few bursts,
That determined the lumbering bomber's fate.

Used all their guns bare,
Until their birds tumbled from the air,
Enflaming the beast here,
Enflaming the beast there,
Cutting the army to shreds.
But then, the enemy's backup came around,
Diving at them, their warbirds cutting through,
The brave aviators.
They recoiled from the warriors
Dodging and weaving.
They flew back, but not
Not the valiant twenty.

Enemy to the right of them,
Enemy to the left of them,
Enemy behind them
Fired at by shot and shell,
Stormed at by the enemy,
While hero and warbird fell from the sky.
They who had fought so well,

Storming the enemy with shot and shell,
Came back from the sky of hell,
Protecting their homeland,
While hero and warbird fell from the sky,

When can their glory fade?
O', the courageous battle they put up,
Defending us from certain death.

Honour the heroes!
Honour the protection they gave!
Honour them!

Harry Gu (9)

Dream Upon A Rainforest

I drift off into a peaceful sleep,
Into a dream I wish to keep,
The trees of lush green,
Much better than from a screen,
The trickling after from the waterfall,
I decide to jump in with a cannonball!
There are pink dolphins and birds of all kinds,
I think I really have lost my mind.

It's the most beautiful sight I have ever seen,
It's better than any other place I've been,
But of course, this is only a dream,
I had to wake up, which made me not so keen,
This could be the last time I see this place,
It went by at such a fast pace.

I wait to hear the sound of my alarm,
I wake up and it's nice and calm,
I look forward to my dream tonight,
I hope it doesn't give me a fright.
But this was the best dream I have ever had!

I wish every dream is like this one,
For many nights to come.

Emilia Parasyri (12)

Cloud

I am seen as air.
I am seen as smoke and air.
I am not solid.
I am sometimes seen as lifeless, stormy or uninteresting.
But I am much more.
More than you may see.
For you are down there and I am up here.
I see life.
I am life.
I can see you and your kind.
I see your ways. Your farms. Your foods.
Forests, cities, houses.
Deserts, mountains and valleys.
I see all things on my long-lasting journey.
I know secrets whispered in the wind.
I know myths and legends from centuries past.
I have no mind of my own, though wise I am.
I am not alone - my brethren and sistren are beside me.
There are thousands, millions of us around the world,
But some I may only meet once.
We are protectors; we gaze upon you either night or day.

We do not rest.
Shielding you from the sun's bright, burning blaze.
We are your guardians. Protectors.
Although we cannot do much and we are very sorry for that.
If we are sorrowful, we may cry down rain, maybe scream out thunder.
If we are perplexed, it may hail.
If we are proud of you (which we always are) it may snow - to give you fun.
In the fog, we are drifting down to murmur, 'Hello'.
Now, I am deeply sorry to those who experience drought.
We're not angry at you and we know you need rain,
But we must follow the path where the wind takes us.
I know it doesn't make sense but even I cannot control nature.
We are all unique. Just like you.
We come in all shapes and sizes.
All with our own knowledge.
But we all know one thing...
As God's creation, we couldn't have asked for a better job than this.
There is so much more I wish to tell you, but I must now go.
But if we someday meet - either on mountain, or in the fog -

Or if we never meet at all, remember this...
We are seen as air.
We are seen as smoke and air.
But we are much more.

Isaac Jones (10)

The Long-Lost Medal

I dreamt of...
A great big ocean with a little girl swimming
The ocean is massive with colourful reefs
Light I can see
A long-lost medal in the depths of the sea
That no one can seem to find
A very precious gold medal from the Olympics games far behind
Explorers, divers and scientists have come and gone
But they left with none
A little girl from another place
Had a dream to find it
She swam and swam and swam
Until she lost her breath
But her eyes lit up when she saw a small glimmer
Sparkling so bright like it was a star or a full moon
Excited, elated and ecstatic
The little girl took hold of the medal with two hands
Raised above her and floated up to the surface of the water
Out of breath and tired but held onto it tight
Eyes wide open, holding onto the blanket and sweating
It was simply a dream.

Zaynab Nadat (5)

Dream On!

Trapped in a cage
In the Stone Age
With a gorilla, a giraffe
And my friend

The cage was so tall
And I was so small
How was this
Story gonna end?

I thought we were doomed
I thought we were toast
Until above me I saw
Some leaves

They were leaves of banana
Banana leaves
Which I asked the giraffe
To retrieve

We used the leaves for flight
The silly gorilla might
Have decorated his with
Bananas

But soon, we were flying
(I felt like happy crying)
And on our way
To Eastern Ghana

We were almost there
Wind in our hair
When we landed
By a school

And I wasn't surprised
That day when I realised
Stealing money
Was a no-no rule

I was in the office of a teacher
Apparently called Ms Preacher
Nicking money
Off her desk

Then, there I was
Running down corridors
With a teacher
Calling me a pest

Now I was stuck
I'd used all my luck

This must have been
The end

Then my ankle got fractured
And I would have been captured
If it wasn't for
My heroic friend

She grabbed me by the arm
Causing me no harm
And dragged me all the way
To the exit

Then we got out the doors
Slamming them with force
Saying "That was all
Rather hectic!"

I know it's bizarre
But we rode the giraffe
To a nearby shop
On the hill

And not to gloat
But we bought a nice boat
(It was called the
Seafaring Will)

We heaved it to shore
Which was rather a bore
But soon we were
All aboard

And then we were off
Sailing across
The vast Atlantic
To discover more...

Ruby Gibbons (10)

The Black Violet

I remember when I was very small,
Vines and trees that reached ever so tall,
But when I went to the other side of the wall,
I saw my whole world suddenly fall,
Everything except the black violet.
My rainbow of hope filled up my heart,
Yet the violet turned black and spread apart,
Everything turned dark, it crumbled in front of my eyes,
The true world is nothing but deceit and lies,
It omitted all I had,
Everything except the black violet.
Roses are red,
Violets are black,
Those you trust the most,
Could stab you in the back,
And kill everything,
Everything except the black violet,
The black violet feeds off greed,
And starts off as a seed,
Of anger, hatred, fear and worry,
And sprouts into a toxic weed,
Planted deep into our minds,
And takes you away from everything,

Everything except the black violet,
Caged in its obsidian leaves,
The black violet takes over the plants and trees,
And trapped me and showed its blade-like thorns,
And it took my heart and ripped it as I mourned,
It tore everything I knew,
Everything except the black violet,
I folded my shadow,
And looked into the sky,
But then the black violet,
Enticed and ate me from the inside,
And burned all I loved,
Everything except the black violet,
Soil as red as blood,
A stem as green as arsenic,
Leaves as black as charcoal,
And petals as dark as the depths of my mind,
And a wall as brown as blood,
A heart as empty as an attic,
And a name that has the colour of night itself,
It controlled everything I owned,
Everything except the black violet,

Everyone has their own black violet,
We just need to learn to control it,

Before it controls you,
And everything,
Everything except the seed of the black violet.

Muaz Abdullah (11)

Dream World

Sometimes I'm glad I'm not alive in my dreams,
Fighting the monsters, or facing my fears,
Blood or horror or sewing up seams,
Working like horses year after year.

But this is not all - there's much more to come,
Being held hostage, a shed for a house,
Seeing a spider even swallowing gum,
Losing my friends and killing a mouse.

But then I suppose there are good dreams too,
When pain or fighting all disappear,
Relaxing all day - too good to be true!
Never a question that's left unclear.

Going on holiday, trees dancing in the breeze,
Doing an exam, got sixty out of sixty!
Driving to town and then a shopping spree,
Meeting my friends and getting a kitty.

If dreams didn't exist, I don't know what I'd do,
They influence me and that is certainly true!

Cynthia Guo (12)

Among The Stars

In a world of wonder and delight,
Where magic fills the air each night,
There lies a place of joy and awe,
A place where dreams take flight and draw.

The circus tent stands tall and proud,
Its colours bright, its music loud.
Inside, performers live their art,
Capturing every beating heart.

Acrobats soar high above,
Twisting, turning, filled with love.
Clowns bring laughter, smiles abound,
Their antics echoing all around.

The ringmaster commands the show,
His voice strong, his presence glows.
He introduces each act with flair,
Building excitement in the air.

Lions roar and tigers prowl,
Daring feats that make us howl.
Trained elephants march in line,
Their grace and power truly divine.

The trapeze artists swing and soar,
Their courage shining more and more.
They leap and twist with perfect grace,
A breathtaking sight to embrace.

The jugglers toss their balls on high,
Their hands a blur against the sky.
Each catch and throw a work of art,
A rhythm that stirs the very heart.
The tightrope walker takes their stand,
Balancing with steady hand.
They walk across the thin, taut line,
A feat that seems almost divine.

Clad in sequins, sparkles bright,
Dancers twirl into the night.
Their movements fluid, graceful, light,
A mesmerising, stunning sight.

The music swells, the lights aglow,
The magic of the circus show.
A world of wonder, joy and cheer,
A place where dreams are always near.

So come one, come all, and join the fun,
Step right up, the show's begun.

In the circus, dreams come true,
A place where magic waits for you.

Harleigh Trask (10)

The Red Planet

The red planet floated alone, its closest neighbour thousands of miles away.
Suspended in an obscure, barren universe, its seclusion grew; the only thing filling the desolate space around were raging balls of fire.
With its climate uninhabitable, the only objects roaming its surface with blood-red rocks, which would crumble into dust touch.
The unbearable heat radiating from its core would incinerate human skin from even the greatest of distances it was so elegant yet so perilous.
However, this planet faced a problem destruction.
Gazing down with fiery anguish at its cousin, it realised its fate had been sealed.
The destruction of earth would soon become its destruction.
The fate of earth would soon become its fate.
Humans would destroy it.
But until then, it floated alone.

The red planet floated alone;
Mars floated alone.

Katarina Dorian (11)

My Dog Dottie And Our Friends

As I was staring out of my bedroom window
With dinky Dottie, I looked out at the beautiful spring meadow.

I said to Dottie, "Shall we go for a walk?"
Dinky Dottie, the talking doggy, said, "I'm too tired to even talk."

So, instead, we got cosy, watched some cartoons on the telly,
We curled up with our blankets and we munched on popcorn and jelly.

In the morning, we were up bright and early.
Ready to go to the flowery spring meadow and find a magical stone that's pearly.

In the spring sun, the swaying trees,
The change of seasons with a steady breeze.

Then who do we see?
But my fantastic best friend, Penelope!

We were both walking our faithful dogs,
Running through the woods, jumping over mossy logs.

We were having so much fun,
That we forgot all about our healthy lunch

Watching the blossom from the trees fall,
Penelope spotted a pearly ball!

We followed this ball that rolled with the wind.
We looked at each other with our huge, big grins.

Our dogs running free,
We hid behind trees.

Then, we looked up and, oh no!
We got lost; we didn't know where to go.

Dottie looked up and told us, "Don't worry.
I'll get us home; we'll be there shortly."

Dottie sniffed with her shiny black nose
Weaving back and forth and away she goes

Before we know it, we are home safe and sound
I'm sure glad Dottie was there to lead us homeward bound.

Jessica Taylor (8)

When I'm Queen

When I grow up, I'm going to be the queen,
First, I'll make brothers illegal,
All sweets and chocolates will be healthy,
And everyone will own a pet seagull,
And when I'm queen,
Farting won't be smelly,
The sun will forever shine,
And you can always watch telly,
Soon I'll be queen,
And bananas won't go mushy and brown,
Nettles won't sting,
And you can eat upside down,
Yes, I'll be queen,
And toilet seats must all be comfy,
Hotels must supply Nutella,
And mattresses will never be lumpy,
When I'm queen,
There will be no such thing as 'bedtime',
Or being told what to do,
And entering my room will be a punishable crime,
As the queen,
It won't matter if your room's a mess,
It doesn't matter if you sleep in till ten,

And nobody can tell you how to dress,
And when I'm queen,
There will be no flu,
People won't die too young,
No one will suffer from diabetes type two,
And as queen, I'll ensure,
That there will be no war or fighting,
There will be no unfairness,
No pinching, no biting,
As the queen,
I'll have ALL the power,
I can change all the rules,
Like driving at 20 miles per hour,
Finally, when I'm queen,
Along with all my other laws,
Kids won't do anything,
And parents will do all the chores!

Yvetta Dixon (12)

The Dreamer's Odyssey

In the quiet of twilight, the dreamer sails,
A vessel of moonbeams and whispered tales.
Across the vast expanse of star-strewn skies,
They chase elusive constellations with wide eyes.

Their ship, woven from threads of forgotten wishes,
Glides through nebulous seas, where time swishes.
Each ripple carries echoes of ancient lore,
And the dreamer steers toward uncharted shores.

Islands of imagination rise from the deep,
Emerald forests where secrets and shadows sleep.
The dreamer steps ashore, barefoot on stardust,
Seeking fragments of truth, love and wanderlust.

In the Garden of Whispers, roses bloom,
Their petals inscribed with verses of doom.
Yet the dreamer plucks hope from thorny stems,
Weaving garlands to wear like diadems.

Mountains of memory loom in the distance,
Their peaks kissed by dawn's golden insistence.
The dreamer climbs, fueled by longing and grace,
To touch the sky's hem and glimpse eternity's face.

At the edge of infinity, they pause and breathe,
Surveying the cosmos - a celestial wreath.
And as morning paints the canvas anew,
The dreamer whispers, "I am stardust too."

For dreams are bridges to realms unknown,
Where the heart finds solace, and seeds are sown.
And the dreamer, forever adrift on this sea,
Sings lullabies to the moon, their silent plea.

Zlata Livtchak (9)

Flying Above

Fairy Tucci was the tiniest fire engine in town.
The other engines were brave and strong
They were never scaredy-cats

Their sirens were glowing pink
They sounded like motorbikes
Heard from far and wide

Emergency! Emergency!
Only the strongest engine could help
Fairy was left behind
Sad and tired
Of never feeling good enough

Closing her eyes
She looked up to the night sky

Above was a shooting star
Glistening blue
She made a wish

"I wish I was a hero."

She whispered to the star
Then closed her eyes

Emergency! Emergency!
The team needed all the engines to help

Fairy hot, excited, it was her time to save the day

The tower was high, the fire was fierce
The engines were lost and could not help

Fairy stepped forward...
She closed her eyes...
She held her breath...

Suddenly, her wheels felt light like clouds
She lifted off the floor
The other engines cheered her on

"Fairy! Fairy! Fairy!"

Carefully, she put out the fire
Rescuing a little girl and her frightened puppy

That day, Fairy became a hero
She would never feel lonely again

Now, the tiniest fire engine was the biggest hero after all.

Ethan Nason (7)

A Frightening Night

It was dark and gloomy, with howling winds.
As I entered the mansion, a gust of wind swept through the air, slamming the doors shut. I couldn't shake off the feeling that I was being watched; the sound of whispers echoed from the corners of the room. My heart raced even faster with every step I took as I made my way through the dimly lit hallway.
The floorboards groaned beneath my feet and the walls seemed to whisper secrets of the past. Suddenly, a candle across the room flickered, illuminating a portrait on the wall. As I looked closer, I saw the face of a woman with a crooked smile spread across her face and her bloodshot eyes. Goosebumps prickled on my skin as I realised she was real, and I wasn't imagining things. *I'm not alone!* a voice screamed inside my head.
Shivers ran down my spine faster than a bolt of lightning, as I stood there horrified, her footsteps echoing through the empty halls. The air grew heavier, suffused with an eerie stillness, my chest tightened as I shivered in fear. Suddenly, a door creaked open by itself, revealing a staircase that descended into a dark murky abyss. With a mix of fear and curiosity, I took a deep breath submerging into the unknown, unaware of the horrors that awaited me.

My heart pounded harder as I went deeper inside. The staircase seemed endless as I drew deeper away from the safety of light...

Mya Das (11)

Once Upon A Dream

I went to sleep, but what I
Didn't know: something was going
To happen to *me!*

I was walking peacefully, holding
A bag of sweets until I saw
A shiny glass and I was curious
To see what it was, but when
I picked it up, I was scared
Because it was rattling and out came
Smoke, it was so heavy, I
Dropped it.

I picked it up again and, surprisingly,
It was a genie.
He said,
"You have three wishes in a row,"
He told me to either say yes or no
And I said, "Yes, of course, bro!"

I said my first wish is for the
War to end, whether in Gaza
Or Ukraine or anywhere, my
Second wish is to fly around

The whole world and my third
Wish is to stop any suffering of children,
No hunger,
No thirst,
No fears,
No tears,
Spread peace around the world
And I hope to see children full of happiness
And joy-ness.

"Are you sure you want that?"
"Yes, yes, yes," I said rapidly.

"Okay, excellent choices you have made,
You picked wisely and may these wishes come true."
"Yay, I am so happy, best day *ever!*"
But then I woke up, finding out
It was all just a *lovely dream*,
Sadly, it wasn't real.

Forqan Omar (11)

The Llama And The Star

Once upon a time
There once was a llama sitting in his pyjamas
Looking at the sky and the stars
"Star, star, I wonder what you are,
Just looking at you so far,"
Sang the llama.
And then he said, "Let's go by trains,
Let's go by planes, just travelling around the world."
"So, I see what you mean,
And I see what you see,
I want you to shine down on me."
So said the llama, "Please can you shine down on all of us?
Because I'll give you a pumpkin,
And I'll give you a dumpling,
And you're a little munchkin,
Because you are so kind."

And the star sang sweetly in the air,
"Oh, oh, oh, no, no, no,
That's not how it goes,
That's how I've been,
Please will you forgive me,
I won't forget you and you won't forget me,

And you're plus and equals and your times fly by,
When you grow up into the storm,
Then you will know the chimps and chickens
Then I will learn space, and you will learn about space,
And then you and I will just live in harmony.

And the llama said, "I'll turn into a watermelon,
And you'll turn into a lemon."

And the star said, "Hey, that's not fair because watermelons are tastier than lemons."

And so, the llama sat in its pyjamas, eating a banana, just staring at the sky.

Elise Real-Slavicky (7)

A Dream

In my bedroom where it is dark and silent
My dream comes true in my sleep.

There lies a sapphire bus waiting for me
Who is as fast as lightning for me
It takes me to the illuminating moon
Who has a cheesy grin on her face
Now I have arrived to the moon
I might be as well the first kid on the rocky stone
I spot some mythical creatures from my imagination
That are the coolest things I've ever seen
Suddenly, the moon shakes under me
Now thinking what to do!

The sphere ball cracks under me and
I end up in a frightening forest
That is in the middle of space
What should I do, what do I do?
I think in my lifeless head
I might have ended in an unfortunate nightmare
I run and run through the depths of the gloomy forest
As well as I find a rainbow, candy castle
When I enter the mystical castle
I find a magical, mysterious unicorn

It seems that it is very friendly
And it also offered me to take me to my sweet home
Just then, I found out it created my dreams
Why is it a unicorn that created my dreams?

After some time, I finally got home
But then, I woke up on my bed
A bit strange?
Oh well, now I have to get ready for today's plan.
A dream.

Tanvi Kuncham (10)

The Fantasy Prairie

There's cotton candy grass
My toes are itching as I pass
Suddenly, it starts raining
But it's candy, all different ones

I popped a candy in my mouth, and one more
I think it will do something, I hope for sure
And it did, wings started to form
Whoosh! Off I went! I thought I was flying to Kent

But it was a prairie instead, full of flowers
I found myself flying over it for hours
It was a dazzling place, other animals were flying too
A leopard, a deer, a dog and a cow saying *moooo*

I landed and found a café run by a rabbit
Her name was Brauny Mabbit
Working there was also a llama named Hama
A gnu named Shmoo
And an ape dressed in a cape

An antelope named Shlubedub posing as a skateboarder
Came up to me to take my order

I'll have butterfly toast with unicorn sprinkles, fairy-dust salt on porcupine needles
It all tasted divine with a little bit of red panda wine

It was getting late, I had to go
I flapped my wings and bid farewell
Lovely meeting all of you, especially my new friend Shmoo
It's time to wake up and start my day
I loved my time at the fantasy prairie, I do hope to come back some way

Sarah Dadusc-Sade (11)

Fantasy Daydreams/Fantasy Nightmares

In a land of jade-green grass,
Hundreds of fantastical creatures pass.
Pegasi, honeybunnies, dragons too,
The dragon scales coloured a vivid blue.
All of the honeybunnies' fur the same,
All as soft as an angelic unicorn's mane.
I see the Pegasi soaring high,
Their majestic white wings beating in the sky.
Pink candyfloss clouds swimming in the fresh air,
Fairies bowing down to their fairy queen heir.
Ballerinas put on a show for all to see,
Doing jetes beneath the gleaming sugarplum tree.
Soon, I'm whisked away from this magical land,
Back to the microscopic room where I stand.

In a land of jet-black grass,
Hundreds of petrifying creatures pass.
Witches, ogres, goblins too,
The goblins' skin a dreary blue.
All the ogres' warts the same,
All as hot as a searing flame.

I see the witches soaring high,
Their dilapidated brooms orbiting in the sky.
Grey, dingy clouds swimming in the smoky air,
Serpents bowing down to their serpent king heir.
Zombies put on a show for all to see,
Swaying beneath the opaque, dule tree.
Soon, I'm whisked away from this ghastly land,
Back to the immense room where I stand.

Tabitha Wilson (10)

Once Upon Addyson's Dream

Life is like a fairy tale with all its love and care
It can also be the villain who wants nothing but despair
Maybe life has been hard on you; the one you love has passed
But I promise you this, my friend, the pain will never last
You didn't lose your slipper on the stair at the golden ball,
You didn't get your perfect prince so easily at all
You can't sing to birds and make them fly directly to your feet.
Maybe you got the old witch who is turning up the heat.
Maybe you are trapped in a tiny, little tower
You can never heal yourself with that special little flower.
Maybe you lost your arrow shooting at the perfect target
Or you sold your voice to the sea witch on dark market
But whenever you're upset or have a tear upon your face,
Just remember you are loved, no matter if you win the race.
Just remember this if you remember nothing more

There is always opportunity behind the wooden door.
Just pick the happy route with joy and full of laughter
Then maybe you don't need that little happy ever after.
So, I leave you with a message of nothing like despair
Don't let life be the villain, choose happiness and care.

Addyson Bishop (12)

Delightful Dreamland

Tick tock, tick tock goes the clock,
As the bells chime the hour.
And above me,
The night begins to tower.

I close my weary eyes,
And kiss the day my goodbyes.
I start to slumber deep,
And soon I fall asleep.

Even though I lie in my bed,
Adventures are juddering to a start in my head.
Then, all of a sudden, with a *bang*,
I get dropped into my imaginary land.

There is the sight of candyfloss clouds,
Primroses speaking aloud,
Majestic mixed-up creatures soaring through the air,
And fiery phoenixes nesting in my hair.
Fantastical and frenetic,
Familiar yet frightening,
I don't know which way's up and which way's down,
This is a fantasy and nonsense-filled town!

But soon I am awoken from my wild dream,
As the sun's rays begin to beam.
The alarm clock once again rings,
And the morning chorus bird sings.

I really hope that my dreams transport me to that world again,
I wonder where other children's dreams take them
So, before you start to take a rest,
Try to imagine your world at its very best.

Elizabeth Osborne (11)

In The Face Of Darkness

Breathing heavily, with a tightness in my chest,
My finger hovering over the light switch,
I was preparing to overcome my fear of the dark,
This was going to be my ultimate challenge.

Could I do it? My friends said, "No!"
They showed little faith in me,
But I'm a winner and a fighter.
I told myself I can, and I will.

Click - darkness descended in an instant.

My spine tightened... all I felt was...
A black cloak over me, smothering me.
My mind raced... all I imagined was...
A cunning criminal hiding in the shadows.
My vision blurred, all I felt was...
Uneasy, as if I was being watched like a hawk hunting down its prey.

Fighting my feelings of fear,
I forced myself to act like a warrior in the heat of battle.
I always took control in my dreams,

Put the fear of the dark side to one side.
Crush the dread and stride onward to the great unknown.

In the corner of my eye, there was a glimmer
Of light from a lonely star,
Making me realise that there is nothing to fear about the dark.
Because it's all just in your mind.

Lucas Brand (10)

A Life In The World

I know a school which is great
Do I love it? It's the big debate
Maths and English, they're the best
But I also really love the rest
There are so many arts and crafts to do
Teachers in the playground, there are only really a few

I know a home which is great
Do I love it? It's the big debate
Games and Nintendo are the best
But I also really love puzzles and the rest
There are so many card games and eating to do
Parents in the kitchen, there are only really a few

I know a park which is great
Do I love it? It's the big debate
Climbing and trees are the best
But I also really love plants and the rest
There's so much walking and playing to do
Fences in the ground, there are only really a few

I know a family which is great
Do I love it? It's the big debate
Aunties and uncles are the best

But I really love cousins and the rest
There are so many parties and outings to do
People in the car, there are only really a few

I know a world which is great
Do I love it? It's the big debate.

Ted Kander (10)

Grief

A veil over your eyes,
Misting the world, masking your joy
And distorting your bliss until it shrivels away into the ashes of your spirit.

Shards of your soul, just ripped from your grasp,
Memories fade into the shadows
And hope seems to be a mere fantasy.

Illusions of wonder and love,
Yet pain is a relentless wave of misery,
Engulfing you in bitter regret.

Clouds envelop the sky in a lifeless grey,
Cloaking the sun in a dismal haze of monotony.
You watch the flowers wither away,
The beauty of spring dissipating before you.
When the flame of youth is extinguished,
And the last sands evade the hourglass,
You realise...

Grief is reverberating joy,
It is the resounding bliss of the memories you have shared, the love you have known, the smiles you have gifted.

Grief is precious.
It is to be treasured - the kin of your emotions.
It is the surge of reminiscence; it is an unparalleled warmth between you.
Love is what makes us who we are.
He is still living, somewhere in your soul, a part of you.
Nobody is gone forever.

Penelope Gilbert (11)

A Screen Isn't As Green

The grass on a screen
Isn't as green
As it is in real life
And it's a knife
To my heart to see kids on screens going by
So I cry,
"Why don't you stop and look around?"
But all they hear is the sound
Of their games on their phone
I feel like a queen upon her throne
When I see nature at its best
Then, I set out on a quest
To make people see the wonders of the world
But people seem to have forgotten how ivy curled
And turn their eyes red with silly things
They've forgotten what a bird sounds like when it sings
I try so hard but really I like screens as well
But I soon remember the smell
Of lavenders when they bloom
I hate how cars vroom
And destroy our air
It's just not fair
So, my dream

Is to beam
A light of hope
So that plants can cope
I love plants
So do ants
I love nature
So, I hate when they are in danger
Help me help them
And you'll be as nice as a gem.

Mahdiyyah Ahmed (10)

Space Wonders

In the vast expanse where stars ignite,
A cosmic dance in eternal flight,
Where galaxies swirl in hues of bright,
I'll make a poem of galactic might,

In the silence, where planets roam,
Each a speciality in the cosmic time,
In the void symphony finds its home,
A timeless epic, yet to be known,

Through the velvet dark, the comets soar,
A celestial prance, forevermore,
In the cosmic balance, the planets evermore,
A tale of wonder, forevermore,

In the heart of the universe, mysteries reside,
Black holes beckon with a pull so wide,
Neutron stars in their brilliant stride,
In the cosmic space, they preside,
So, let this poem traverse the expanse,
Where galaxies spin in a cosmic dance,
In the boundless void, we take our chance,
To marvel at the cosmic trance,

For the realm of stars collide,
Imagination's bounds, they're defined,
In the poetry of space, we confide,
A universe of dreams forever tied.

Ayati Pal (11)

Beneath The Vast And Endless Sky

Where dreams take wing and spirits fly,
A tapestry of stars above,
Weaves tales of loss, of hope, of love.

In silence deep and whispers light,
The moon does dance with pure delight,
And in its glow, the world seems right,
A beacon in the velvet night.

The rivers hum a gentle tune,
A melody beneath the moon,
They speak of journeys far and wide,
Of secrets deep where truths reside.

The mountains stand, both proud and tall,
Their peaks like giants never fall,
They hold the weight of time untold,
And stories new and stories old.

So, take a breath and close your eyes,
Let your heart soar, let your spirit rise,
For in this world of wonder vast,
Each moment's precious, none shall last.

Embrace the beauty, hold it tight,
For life is a poem, in the night,
A fleeting verse, a transient light,
A gift of love, a pure delight.

Mehreen Azim (12)

Create A Dream World

I pulled my blanket over me and fell asleep,
Soon, I was deep in a dream,
I had washed up on this lush island,
Filled with palm trees overlooking the ocean,
Which is as blue as the sky,
It was paradise!

The ocean water gleamed in the sunlight,
Creating a magical aura in the sky,
The sand was bright yellow on the edge of the island,
I was in awe,
I was astonished unsure where I was,
Where am I?
Was I lost? I asked myself.

A pink dolphin jumped out of the azure-blue ocean,
I was in shock,
It was magical,
I went diving into the ocean,
Wanting to play with the dolphin,
After an enjoyable half an hour,
I got out of the water and I felt so tired.

I lay down on the sand with the bright sun shining over me,
Seconds later, I was awake in my bedroom,
Not on the island,
It hit me, I was in a dream,
I really enjoyed it even if it wasn't real,
I was tired, so I pulled the covers over me,
As I wanted to get some sleep.

Dhruv Maheshwari (11)

The Phantoms

Mud and ashes cover the ground,
in the eerie graveyard, there is no sound,
But there, in the darkness,
The phantoms dwell,
Guarding the gates between
Earth and Hell,
So cold, they make ice out of dew,
So transparent,
The human eyes see right through,
They soar past the old shacks,
And glide through the grass,
Whistling an eerie tune,
And spreading melancholy as they pass,
They're not the creatures you'd expect,
They don't give frights for fun,
But life is what they really desire,
Each and every one,
They are not decayed human souls,
But prisoners from the underworld,
A burden upon them, a shower of sorrow,
A mystery yet to be unfurled.

Mud and ashes cover the ground,
In the eerie graveyard, there is no sound,
But there, in the darkness,
The phantoms dwell,
Guarding the gates between
Earth and Hell.

Amaan Mughal (11)

Cake And Squid

When I say I don't dream,
People respond with, "You're absurd!"
They say I just don't remember them,
So, I tell them a story about curd,

"I once had a dainty curd cake,
Which caused me to have a dream,
It really was rather odd,
It was all about cake and cream,

I flew across an ocean,
Gazing down at glorious squid,
When I flew into a rundown shop,
With cakes that cost a quid!

I really was getting hungry,
So I flew in and sat myself down,
I called the waitress over,
And found my last half crown,

The lady asked how much I had,
So I lied and answered, "One quid,"
But sadly she saw right through me,
And threw me in with the squid."

I never really got over it,
Dreams still freak me out,
So if you ask me for a dream,
I'm afraid I'll scream and shout.

Emma Nicholas (12)

The Magical Treehouse

In my garden, there's a big tree,
It holds a treehouse built by me.
But in the day, it is small.
In my dreams, it's big and tall.

At night, when I get put to bed,
Dreams fill my head,
I wake up and my treehouse is glowing so bright,
Taking me to dreams each night.

I fly out of my treehouse, with wings like a fairy,
Then, I see an ugly beast so big and hairy.
The flowers start dancing in the moonlight,
I was so astonished, it was a beautiful sight.

I play netball with my friends,
The fun and games never end.
We laugh and run, we pass and cheer,
In dreams, everything feels near.

But then, the sun begins to rise,
I rub my sleepy, tired eyes.
The treehouse comes to a pause,
Still, to this day, I wonder why this is caused.

So, I can't wait until tonight,
For the treehouse to become so bright.

Effie Ellis (10)

Dreams

A dream slips through an invisible window crack,
Slowly tiptoeing up to your bed
Creeping into your head, a dream can be a wonderful thing or
Something dark and gloomy.

It could take you to an endless world,
Bubbling rivers past cosy cottages,
Up in space, among the stars
Through a black hole!
Dreamscapes surrounding you.

But, in a dark space in your mind bad dreams enter,
Scary monsters that bring no joy,
A dragon with fiery breath,
An eagle swooping down
Injecting sharp claws into your shoulder, carrying you away.
Falling from an unstable cliff,
Being chased by shadows.

Chase away bad dreams, it's all that you can do...
Dreams will always tiptoe through your window on any starry night,

When you wake, all you'll hear
Is the gentle breeze blowing in the morning.

Elise Thomas (8)

Last Goodbye

It seems this goodbye is forever,
That I won't get another hello.
People are already telling me to 'move on from the past'.
Yet I am standing in it and I refuse to go to the future without it.
I've tried to lie to people,
Tell them, "I'll make new friends."
But the words refuse to leave my mouth.
So, when that goodbye does happen, I'll keep my head held high,
Because I believe in the future that they will find me again,
So, with difficulty, I tell you,
A dream, but a nightmare now, it's coming true,
That I'll leave my friends and my school too.
But maybe, just maybe,
This is all a dream,
And I will wake up tomorrow,
My friends with me,
So, even though I know that's not true,
I'll keep my head raised high, knowing I'll see them all soon.
Goodbye!

Isla Massie (11)

The Cat That Was A Magician

This incredible magician's name is Elodie!
She is about as small as a dice.
Oh, that is a bit funny, isn't it?
Because she is very familiar with them too!

From her ears to the top of her tail, she is a mix of brown and black!
When she sees a fire, she is the one who will put it out.
Elodie is a mystery cat.

Her nickname is 'Boss' because she acts like one around here!
When she sees a deck of cards, she is the one who will win that game.
She can also run on a tiniest rail.
You really are the boss around here!

If she is invited into a mansion, she will crush everything she sees to bits.
She will also sit on the roof to relax!
Maybe I should actually go, "Bye-bye, Elodie, I've got to go now!"
This will be our little secret, as I didn't actually need to leave!

Lily Cryer-Richard

This Is Me, I'm A Traveller

I flew away,
For long I stayed,
In a place I don't belong,
However, for this place I have longed,
People say this place is full of sunshine and life,
But the air feels cold and the place feels dull,

I feel like a stranger,
In this world I fell into,
I feel lost, trapped like I... fell into darkness,
How I long for the light, my home,
I find myself calling for home,
But there is no one to hear my cries,
That's when I realise,
I'm entirely alone,

It feels like this place is running away from me,
I chase after it again and again,
But I can't keep up, so I keep trying,
I run as fast as I can, but so will the world,
So, I stop chasing after the place where I'll never belong,
I fly back to home,
And I see this is really where I belong.

Fatima Nabeeha (12)

Nightmare Or Dream?

As I tuck away into bed,
My head drifts into another world,
I slowly walk by mystical fairies,
And massive dragons that are indeed scary,
I delightedly dance around chocolate-covered fields,
I devour sweets until my tummy squeals.

Suddenly, something falls from the sky,
I look around and wonder why,
Then, I hear an evil, deafening cry,
A dark shadow emerges from crumbled gingerbread,
Spikes hanging from its back,
Its red eyes flooded with hunger and dread,
I watch as it swallows the town,
And our people frown,
But just then the sun shines bright,
And the creature vanishes into the shadows with fright.

My eyes open, wide and I jump out of bed,
I look out at the window to see the morning sun rays,
I stumble to the floor and think to myself,
Nightmare or dream? This is very weird.

Tofunmi Sowanola (11)

Haunted House

I enter a room,
Full of gloom.
Then see blood,
Along with a thud.

Who could it be?
Then, there's a creak,
I shout, "Who's there?"
But they just won't speak.

Could it be a ghost?
I see a spider
Crawling into a bottle of cider.
Something starts emerging from the passageway,
And I was about to dash away.
But I knew I had to be courageous
And not be outrageous.

A head started appearing,
And I kept on fearing;
I kept on wandering
And I knew I couldn't be squandering.

Then...

Its whole body emerged,
And I started to submerge.
Its clothes were torn and ripped apart,
But that was just the start.
His face was like an alien's head, covered in grease and slime,
And his whole body was full of grime,
And his shoes were just unlike mine.

His name was Frankenstein.

Kevin Xu (11)

My Velociraptor

Oh, my velociraptor,
Were you green like a pear?
Were you blue like the ocean?
Were you black like the night?
What colour were you?
My velociraptor,
What colour were your eyes?
Were they yellow like bananas?
Were they red like fire?
Were they pink like flamingos?
What was your movement like?
Did you move fast like a cheetah?
Were you vicious like a cobra?
Were your packs as coordinated as an army?
Were your claws as sharp as swords?
Did you move them as fast as comets?

I will avoid you in the past.
With my time machine, I will drive away your enemies.
Let them no longer say you didn't exist.
You were the monarch of the Cretaceous.

In your packs, you could bring down a T-rex.
My velociraptor,
The past belongs to you.

Jason Medina (8)

The Takeover

This world's plain, and grown-ups are lame,
They always say 'no', so they must go,
Imagine my dream where kids take over
And give this world a new makeover!

Me and my mate will stay up late
Watching movies and drinking smoothies,
Talking about teachers we hate

The next day, I'll go to the zoo,
And buy a sloth and a lizard or two,
I'll buy a sweet treat for them to eat,
While dodging flying monkey poo

I'll wear my hair down,
Leave my undies on the floor
Eat bottles of ketchup,
And join ABBA on tour

If grown-ups want to stay,
They have to follow what I say -
Not muck about in work all day.
You've all forgotten how to play.

You're now in my school
And it's all cray-cray
Follow my rules
And let's play, play, play!

Lyra Thomas (7)

The Space Journey

Five, four, three, two, one, blast-off!
It's the perfect time to set off!
We're going towards space,
We're not in a chase or a race.

Ruby-red, guess where we are!
Yes, you're right, we're on Mars!
We've travelled so far, we need buns,
But we're not here for buns, we need fun!

This one's the biggest, no need to see a picture.
How did you know that we are on Jupiter?
This one's also the heaviest
But it's not the brightest!

Saturn has pretty rings!
Coldness is what Neptune brings!
These planets are full of gases,
Despite this, they have big masses!

We've now reached the Kuiper's belt,
It's really icy, so it won't melt!
We see asteroids, there are a lot,
We look back at the planets and they look like dots!

Jessica Malarini Nirmalan (10)

A Wild Dream

My dreamland is described fun. With iced tea and hot cross buns.
The floor is made of bubblegum. Have a bounce, don't be glum.
Unicorns prance on the clean floor. We all can even soar!
The stars are alive with hope and love. With respect and kindness, nobody is rough.
With libraries galore, where books are alive. This is the place I thrive.
This world is magical, with wands and wizards. With green-scaled lizards.
Trees are made from cotton candy. Animals sing on the ground, which are sandy.
Monsters are kind, not scary. They would rather eat berries.
Animals can go to work and play. They can't just sit and stay all day.
Pokémon are always real. Nobody is going to steal.
One day, I hope this is true and going. I really want people knowing.

Gareth Wong (9)

A Fluff That Says Ruff-Ruff

He is as soft as a cloud,
And he fits in with the crowd.
He's my puppy forever,
And he's very clever.

He knows all his tricks,
And he loves chasing sticks.
He wakes me up gently in the morning,
And comes to my bed without a warning.

He's cute and he's fluffy,
And he looks a bit chuffy.
He gives me kisses,
And he never hisses.

He picks me up from school,
And that is very cool.
He's one of a kind,
And that is so hard to find.

He makes me happy,
And he's sometimes yappy.
He's my joy,
And he's the size of a toy.

His name is Fluff,
And he says, "Ruff-ruff."
I love him to the moon and back,
And I will always treat him with a snack.

He's my bestie for life,
And the sweetest soul alive.

Mia Istakov (8)

What's Your Thing?

My special thing,
It's not gardening,
My friend, Clark,
He tried to help me find my spark,
He said, "Let's make her,
Try to be a baker,"
I don't want to prance around,
And learn to dance,
Maybe it's my chance to make some pants,
Darling, it's not charming,
Or self-alarming,
You could make a note,
About a quote,
Or I could learn to skate,
With my mate Nate,
Learn to bake what's on your plate,
My daughter,
Well, she's an author,
My son,
He's made some iced buns,
That's what he's done,
I could board,
Or try to play a chord,

Or study rocks,
Or knock my socks,
Right off of me,
Or operate a knee,
What could I be...?

Charlotte Dawes (9)

Holiday For A Nightmare

H oliday for a nightmare
O n a cruise through your
L ittle bloodstream
I nnocent is you
D inging bells
A nd taking trains
Y ou are doomed from a dream

F arting is a nightmare's favourite thing to do
O r eating your mind
R etro style taking a taxi

A nd takes itself to another brain

N attering in your mind
I n your mind, it thinks it is time
G etting away by a Mark 3 tank
H itting and bashing your mind
T inkering at your head
M eaning you're still in your bed
A nd you have bad dreams
R icketing your mind
E ating your brain which is a sweet to them.

Hamish Coles (8)

Cloud-A-Corn

High above the clouds, where it's quiet and misty,
I saw a Cloud-a-corn who was very fuzzy.
Was it a dream or was it real?
I wondered how it would feel.
I moved closer to see how it felt,
Closer and closer until I touched its fur pelt.
Her candyfloss-like fur was as soft as wool,
She bit my hair and gave me a little pull.
She snorted on my face but I felt no fear,
Beads in her hair in the shape of a sphere.
Her eyes shone like diamonds sparkling at night,
She neighed very loudly and it gave me a fright.
Her horn was the colour of a colourful rainbow,
Over her shoulder, her hair would flow.
I really love this majestic creature,
I wish I could bring her home.
All the things I could teach her!

Khadijah Arfan Ahmed (11)

A Desert Dream

In the heart of the desert, a beautiful land, there are miles and miles of soft searing sand.
The sun is King Midas' beautiful touch, spreading down gold on the things in its clutch.
Down in the desert, cactuses thrive. But I'm not a cactus, will I survive?
Camels are cool, we all can agree, but they're really not cool when they're spitting at me!
An ocean of sand, endless and vast, I was sailing upon it, my mind as my mast.
I drank from an oasis; it tasted so bitter! It's probably because it was filled up with litter!
In the late hours of night, I lay on a dune, I gazed at the stars, and gaped at the moon.
The moon glimmered down, and the stars shone so bright, I tucked myself in, and then said, "Goodnight!"

Delilah Morrison (9)

Once Upon Their Dream

Once upon Walt's dream,
Came Mickey and Minnie Mouse,
From the everlasting mind of Walt Disney,
Who created over 7,000 characters,
Bringing happiness to the world.

Once upon Stan's dream,
Swung Spider-Man and Captain America,
From the tremendous ideas,
By the creator of over 8,000 warriors,
Saving the lives of the innocent.

Once upon George's dream,
Arose Luke Skywalker and Obi-Wan Kenobi,
Born from the sensational imagination of George Lucas,
Making over 20,000 space explorers,
Starting many terrific galactic adventures.

All these people and many more,
Inspire many dreams to come true,
Along with yours,
Taken off the pillow and into reality.

Mia Ellerington (10)

My Moon And Sun

O' sun, light of my world
I appreciate you
Guiding me in belligerent situations
O' moon, the path of my life
I acknowledge you
Assisting me when tenebrosity captures

Even with the thousands of mistakes I make
You lead me with a forgiving heart
Even with the thousands of troubles I face
You leave me with a delighted smile

When the caliginous sky approaches
You hold me close and say, "Behold, I am with you."
When the terrifying thunder roars
You hug me tight and say, "Behold, I am with you."

O' dear father, sun of my life
O' dear mother, moon of my life
As long as the sun and the moon last
I will love you as the years pass.

Kairos Sunuwar (10)

Earth

E ven though everything looks fine,
A planet is dying, our planet,
R ight now we should get up and act,
T rying on your own won't work,
H elp is what is needed for us and the planet.

O ther than temperatures rising, coral is crumbling,
U nited, we can stop it all,
R obots may be cool, but bees are dying.

P lease help the planet,
L ies are being spread, that we can just sit around,
A nd while we do that, forests are dying,
N ever will the planet die if we help it,
E veryone can help, young or old,
T reating the planet with respect will let us live for years to come.

Alfie Inkster (11)

Adventures Through The Night

In my dreams at night,
I sail through the sea,
That glimmers in the dark,
A perfect sight for me.

I swim around with sharks,
That roam the deepest spots,
Where underwater creatures,
Gather round, there's lots.

I play at different beaches,
And spot a competition,
The biggest sandcastle wins,
Now focus, I'm on a mission.

I battle with some knights,
That ride horses and swipe swords,
I show off all my moves,
To the King of Chestnut Moors.

I have discovered different places,
And gobbled all I can,

I have heard some spooky voices,
I was frightened, so I ran.

But I wake up safe in bed,
Not a single bit of dread,
My dreams are over for the night,
My eyes now open, wide and bright!

Abigail Living (9)

In A Dream

In a dream, a hazy vision
A misty gauze swept away
To reveal a childish dreamland
Echoing with lost wishes

In a dream of a world reborn
Into a new universe
Basking in the light
Of a glowing, new dawn

In a dream of new hopes
Of new beginnings
A flawless perfection
Unachievable, except -

In a dream, of somewhere
Some place, where I could
Be free of the leash
Choking, grasping, strangling

In a dream, where I could
Be safe, be true, be real
In a new reality
That could only ever exist

In a dream, just a dream
A forlorn wish
In a dream, only ever a dream
Echoing with lost hope.

Adeeba Farah (13)

The Vampire's Tale

Many consider me evil,
And that may be partly true.
But I have to eat humans to survive,
As with animals do you.

So, call me what you want,
It depends on point of view.
But I have to eat humans to survive,
As with animals do you.

I have to lurk in the shadows,
You should see the places I'm forced into.
But I have to eat humans to survive,
As with animals do you.

You hate every one of us,
Even though we only number few.
But we have to eat humans to survive,
As with animals do you.

All humans try to injure me,
My diet I certainly rue.
Because I have to eat humans to survive,
As with animals do you.

Benyamin Mustafa (10)

The Following Of The Shadows

As you walk into the shadows
You see yourself as a blurred image
But then it strikes you
Like a lightning bolt
And out of nowhere, you see a different image

You can't explain what or who it is
All you know is that it's something
That isn't still but is moving
You see it creeping across the floorboards
Coming nearer and nearer with a whisper at every step

You hear shouting and screaming
Noise after noise
It follows you *everywhere*
It comes closer and closer until…
It stops

You hear a beeping noise
That will not leave you alone
Suddenly, the image becomes clearer
And you realise that it is…

Francesca Lloyd (11)

Once I Was A Hero

I had a rhyme
When I saw a crime
Was I dreaming
When I heard people screaming?
I saw a broken window
When I saw a statue - wait! It's an actual hero
I thought the hero would save me
But it turned out to be a phony
I saw the police
They were huddled together like a group of geese
It was hard for them to catch the thief
Because they were shaking with grief
I knew it was my time to shine
So the day would become mine
After that, there was a silent crowd
Then, slowly and slowly, it began to get loud
Cheers of happiness rose above
In this beautiful sky, there were lovely doves
I finally saved the day
In the month of May.

Aria Gaberria (9)

If Every Wish Came True

If every wish came true,
I'd wish for a majestic unicorn,
Whose wings would shine with pride,
She'd have a glittery, colourful horn,
And flap her wings whilst I'd enjoy the ride!

I'd wish for a fabulous rocket,
That could fly me to the moon,
Faster and brighter than a comet,
It would take off with a *boom!*

I'd wish to reach the end of the rainbow,
With pots overflowing with gold,
The colours would put on an extravagant show,
Ones I'd never imagined; so vibrant and bold.

Now every morning when I wake,
I think of everything I can do,
All these visions I will not forsake,
Because now I know that dreams really do come true.

Aaliyah Shakoor (10)

My Dragon Dream

Haiku poetry

One day I woke up,
Yawning and feeling hungry,
So I went downstairs.

All of a sudden,
A magic portal appeared,
With fiery dragons.

All of them in space,
From another dimension,
Strange and mythical.

It looked amazing,
I wanted to explore it,
And so I stepped through.

On the other side,
I was floating all around,
Thinking what to do.

Dragons came to me,
They asked me, "Why are you here?"
I said I was lost.

Kindly, they helped me,
And made a portal to leave,
I made it home safe.

Rubbing my red eyes,
I was lying in my bed,
My mum calling me.

Myles Joseph (11)

A Saturday Afternoon In The Sun

I'm sat in my garden, writing this for you
The wind is blowing on my cheeks
The flowers are blooming and the butterflies are dancing in the breeze

The sun is shining
My dog is sheltering from the blazing sun
In the misty, dark shadow of the house

My mum is gardening in the sunlight
Her magical eyes searching the grounds for stray plants like an eagle searching for its prey

My dad is sat in the sun, admiring the flowers and watching the emerald leaves swaying in the breeze

My brother is tottering around listening to an exciting audiobook about magical creatures like dragons with glistening scales and graceful wings.

Estelle Sutton (9)

The Unexpected Gift

A magical gift appeared at my door,
In desperation, I stumbled across the floor.
Within the box, a treasure lay,
A glowing chip, as small as my toy ship's display.

With a tap, the chip came to life,
Swirling me into a world without strife.
Technology danced in a cosmic ballet,
Among ferns that flourished, in a verdant array.

Floating trains and cars took flight,
In a realm where dreams took flight.
This was the world I longed to explore,
Where stars adorned the horizon's core.

Returning home, with a toy car in hand,
Memories of adventure, a journey so grand.
Now safe within my pocket's embrace,
The chip rests, a token of that enchanted place.

Ziyang William Li (9)

Maw And Picky

I dream of you every night,
Maw and Picky together day after day
But especially when you love to play.
I always see you catching mice
I wonder, do they taste nice?
Sometimes you snooze, sometimes you snore.
Sometimes you seem like you're in a war!
Sometimes you're happy, sometimes you're sad.
Sometimes you smell really bad!
But be careful because sometimes they hiss
And sometimes they scratch!
Sometimes they need some sleep.
But the most important thing is I love them both
And that will never change.
So, now let's close the book and say goodnight
And I'll see you in the morning.
That's right!

Etta Jordan (9)

Gibbles' Talent

I stopped and couldn't help but stare
My pet was in the middle of Times Square.
With a saxophone in his hand, it was a thought I had to process.
But I knew this would be a success.
I knelt down and Gibbles looked up at me and stared.
I said, "Who let you out here in the middle of Times Square?"
I looked down at my feet and underneath me was his star.
Is his name really on the Walk of Fame? How bizarre
I am proud of being his owner, it makes me feel good.
Anyway, I thought show me what you can play.
He started one note after the other and this turned out to be a good day.
He jumped into my hand and he knew that I am his number one fan.

Adele Bagdonas (11)

The Flight To Dreamland

Relax, be calm and still,
Release your mind,
As your journey to dreamland begins.
Let your imagination, be the creation of the world you want to see.
Your library of thoughts will guide you here and there.
Creating great confusions, heightening your emotions,
Some feelings you might not even bear.
A single dream can give you a fusion of different thoughts,
Which may inspire, bring humour, fear or despair.
Many spiritual beings, believe dreams give you a message or may come true,
That depends on what you dream of, of course.
But only you can unlock the true secrets of what dreams are truly whispering to you.
So close your eyes, and let's begin,
A new adventure, from deep within.

Meera Jassal (9)

Dream Catcher

When I go to bed at night,
I sometimes worry I'll have a fright,
That my nightmares will give away my dreams,
But there's something waiting to catch the scenes.

I'm hoping that in the middle of the web,
The magical object will protect my head,
And with the feathers hanging on,
It makes a swaying hypno song.

And with the naughties floating away,
The good ones come and save the day!

There are dreams about kittens and no school galore,
And dreams about sweets, I want more, *I want more!*
Now you get the idea about having to sleep,
But don't wake up because nightmares are cheap.

Isabelle Gower (8)

Panda's Playful Prowl

In a forest made of bamboo so tall,
Lived a happy panda, playful and all.
With fur of black and white so bright,
She danced and pranced with sheer delight.

In the jungle of bamboo, she'd roll,
From her bamboo bed, she'd stroll.
Tumbling out with a giggle and a leap,
Her eyes twinkled like stars in sleep.

Playing alone in a make-believe game,
In a hidden spot, she found her fame.
Dreaming of adventures far and wide,
Where friends join her on a joyful ride.

I'll never forget you, my special friend,
Forever together, hand in hand, we'll blend.
In each other's hearts, we'll always stay,
Through every adventure, come what may!

Catherine Li (7)

Hope

I rise and fall like the ocean deep
I'm always joyful and I never weep
I'm true and don't put out the lights
With me, you will reach amazing heights.

You don't see me, but I'm always there
The sound of the song dancing in the air
The candle fighting away the dark
The tree standing firm in the park

A ship sailing safely to the dock
The faithful step to the sturdy rock
I am the milky, moonlit cloud
The flicker of wonder always around.

So, remember all the people who
Have followed their hearts warm and true
It is easier to cope
If you decide to live in hope.

Penelope Hughes (10)

Candy Land

C andy Land is the most amazing place, with chocolate and sweets to stuff your face.
A ll of what you can see is edible and absolutely free!
N ougat, caramel or a strawberry lace, whatever you fancy, it's all over the place.
D iam bar, ice cream marshmallows - the lot!
Y ummy gummy bears that have wings that can fly, they go so high you can see Dubai.

L uscious liquorice, black ones too, red and blue, even ones shaped just like twos.
A ll of the sugar made me hyper, to do cartwheels in a diaper
N ever-ending chocolate streams
D ang it, I woke up, it was all a dream.

Alistair Butterworth (9)

The Magical Beach

Splash.
The salty, sapphire sea danced like a pirouetting
Ballerina... ballerina... ballerina,

Sizzle.
The burning, bright sun shone like a ball of fire in the clear blue
Sky... sky... sky,

Swoosh.
The brilliant breath of the wind was like a whirling
Fan... fan... fan,

Crunch.
The perfect, pretty sand was blown across the ground like particles rolling down a
Hill... hill... hill,

Rustle.
The terrific, towering palm trees stood like a crowd of vivid green
Umbrellas... umbrellas... umbrellas,

And then I woke up.

Jessica Lee (10)

The Land Of Dragons

Once upon a dream, whilst I sleep.
Dragons flew by at the dark of night,
I knew I may have to fight.
Roaring fire and golden sand,
I was not ready for this land.
What shall I do?
Shall I say, "Boo!"?
No, it might scare them away,
Maybe I'll do it another day.
Oh no, I've been spotted,
The dragons approach,
So big they stand, I feel like a cockroach.
But as they get closer, they look scared of me,
How could this be?
I look down, but I'm far from the ground.
I am the biggest, fiercest dragon, glowing red,
Suddenly, I wake up in my cosy bed.

Summer Byrne-Williams (8)

Ballerina

As I enter the long, glittering room,
I see a ballerina,
I see it twirling around
And tiptoeing on her delicate feet ever so often,

I see her leaping across the room,
And it's keeping its balance ever so slightly,
At once, she glared at me,
She tiptoed over to me,
Tiptoe, tiptoe, tiptoe,
She gave me a fright,

She asked me to dance
But I kept holding back
Until she grabbed my arm
And we twirled into the terrific spotlight,
We were leaping together,
Jumping together,
Twirling together,
But I will never forget the day that we met.

Hafsa Shafiq (10)

The Dream

I dream I could fly,
Like a star in the sky.
To travel to the Seven Sisters,
To be adopted and be one of the sisters.
To escape Earth fast,
To escape the grasp.
Just to mill around,
Not to astound.
To show how quickly people can turn around,
To be famous all around.
Suddenly, gravity pulls me down,
I'm as unhappy as a clown.
I like my old home,
But it just doesn't feel like home.
I'm not noticed at school,
I feel like an abandoned tool.
I'm glad to be back in Montly,
Because up in space it was really lonely.
Suddenly, the dream falls out of me,
Because I'm tucked up in bed as safe as can be!

Dylan Sessions (8)

Space Monsters

S leeping soundly at night,
P reparing to give me a fright,
A great, red, fiery, gigantic beast,
C oming to get a good feast,
E ntering my dreams and disturbing my sleep,

M ythical monster from a deep, dark space,
O pening his spaceship, I can see his face,
N ear my bed, he shouts, "Hello!"
S eeing my scared face below,
T ickling my feet to make me giggle,
E verything shakes as I wiggle,
R unning towards his spaceship,
S pace Monster says, "Goodbye, pip!"

Henry Start (9)

The Haunted House

Creepy ghouls round every corner,
A venomous cobra slithers by.
Nothing you can do, monsters creeping up behind you
Yes, an escape! But no! A library maze!
Skeletons chasing you,
Oh no! A dead end, you're doomed!
You fall down, down, down.
Thump! You hit the ground,
You're in a room as black as night.
A mummy limps towards you,
Where to go?
Sweat on your forehead
Don't go back the other way
Straight through a door and outside

Never
Go
In
There
Again.

Violet King (8)

The Bravest Cat Of All

Her golden feline eyes
Dance around in the moonlight
They may not be the prettiest
But they are good enough for me.

Her paws float across the ground
Don't even brush the grass blades
They may not be the fastest
But they are good enough for me

Her smooth tortoiseshell coat
Can slip under the smallest of fences
It may not be the prettiest
But it's good enough for me

She is now overseas
I don't see her anymore
But I still know
She may not be the bravest cat of all
But Tigger is brave enough for me.

Emma Cooper (10)

The Beast

Down below was an icy grave,
The wind whipped my skin,
To nature I was a slave.
The snow had smothered all happiness and light,
I was painstruck and weak,
But I had to fight.
Then, suddenly, beat after another,
A dragon's wing, another thing to discover,
It rose out of the ground, disturbed and awoken.
With other monstrosities that are unspoken.
It searched around in this empty white void,
Its once-luscious home,
Now thoroughly destroyed.
It beat its wings like a solemn salutation,
Leaving its home,
For the next generation...

Alick Patton (11)

The Nightmare

As I laid my head and went to bed,
I didn't know,
I was going to have a nightmare so rare.
In my dream, I was on holiday!
A day with just playing, *hooray!*
We were at the beach,
I was eating a peach.
Then...
Down came a plane and it started to rain,
And my holiday was ruined.
I woke up and looked at a cup
And then I saw a light,
"Right," I said, "straight to bed because now you're just seeing things."
"Phew!" whispered the tooth fairy.
That was close. *Way* too close.

Diana Strepka (9)

The Poem About Roald Dahl

Roald Dahl is the one who inspires me.
He writes many mind-blowing books every time
And thinks about his next piece of work.
He wrote so many books until he died,
He was the best children's author in the world.

I love reading his books
He inspires me to write books of my own.
And grow famous just like Roald Dahl did.

I was really upset when Roald Dahl died
But people will always remember him in their hearts
Forever writing the best books in the world.
He will always remain the best children's author in the world.

Meth Asher (9)

Once Upon A Dream

Once upon a dream
I want to be an author
That will make me stronger
I want to write about space
And it will be ace
About magical creatures
Ones that are teachers
But one creature
One teacher
Named Star
That can travel far
She has galaxy powers
That grows precious flowers
And she can teach for hours
Star is strong
And confident to sing a song
She knows she is amazing
And loves embracing
Everybody loves her
And wants to be her friend
But she knows that her best friend is you.

Lilly Tyler (10)

Through Your Eyes

How can I see through your eyes when your world is so different to mine?
I wish I could do it just for a day, to see the world how you play
To know why you get sad and cry sometimes
To see why the world is so loud
You get angry and mad when you can't say out loud the word that's trapped deep inside somehow
It's too bright
It's too loud
I can't see the world through your eyes
I don't understand, I wish I could
But I will always stand by your side
My brother
My twin
My everything.

Hope Miles (9)

Hurricane

The water thrashes and crashes against the cliffside,
It swirls and whirls into the air, making land a foggy mess.
The land I saw is not what the hurricane withdrew,
People fleeing left and right into the misty distance,
My heart was destroyed like the houses around me,
Families' hearts broken whilst some bones were broken,
The hurricane roared with the strength of a hundred lions,
Children scream and shout for their mums whilst parents are in pools of tears,
When the storm is quiet, a new world is born.

Laurie Roth (9)

How Christina Ran

There were a hundred spiders,
They were like a shield,
Their legs went *click, clack*,
They looked like bats,
They wanted to suck my blood!
Death, pain, poison.

Then, I saw another Christina,
There were two of us,
The other one was an alien!
I began running,
But I felt tired,
I sat down.
My legs said, "Hey!
We want to keep running!"

The alien Christina and the spiders
Were actually my family;
My brother and my mummy!

Christina Lucille Young (4)

A Winter Wonderland Tale

In the winter, there was a house and in the house was a girl,
A girl no one had ever seen before.

No one knows her
No one knows where she came from.

She was extraordinary,
She was mysterious,
She was beautiful, her hair as white as the snow that was dropping in the sky,
Her lips were rosy and as red as blood that was

Coming out of her hand while sewing,
Her skin so fair that
People said she was a goddess for she was the girl from the
Room from the house and from the winter.

Amarachi Obeta (10)

Famous Footballer Gets Lost

It all starts winning a match,
Not of catch,
The fans got a bit carried away,
And went the wrong way,
So, the captain followed them,
But it was the wrong fans,
So, they threw cans,
He got knocked out,
And dreamt about,
Winning the league,
Then getting lost,
Looking everywhere,
Fighting a bear,
He's run ten hours,
He went up a tower,
Opened the wrong door,
On the wrong floor,
Then he woke up,
Getting tucked in by his 'new' pup!

Carter Davis (7)

Once Upon A Dream!

I dream a dream where,
I can be the perfect one.
Building my castles every day
Climbing up the mountains and jumping down the cliffs
I didn't know it was the last one
I wish I could sleep more to dream more
Now I swim in an ice cream fountain where,
There is no place for tears
I want to be free and want to be seen
The sky is full of clouds
I want to dance and twirl
I want to feel like I belong to this magical world of dreams
Always touched by wind and kissed by grace.

Nia Vinod (8)

The Island Of Paradise

Crystal-clear pools of blue
And dense thickets of magnificent clues,

All shine bright and clear
In my vivid dream.

Gushing waterfalls of calm, plunged water,
Flow gently as if in order.

Trees and cottages greet me with glee,
Waves of happiness rocking into me

Soft, yellow rays of the incandescent sun,
Glisten on the scenic mountains when they won.

These are the happenings of my one dream,
All created by my big, blooming brain team.

Shanaya Koul (11)

My Superpower

S uperpowers raging with fright
U nderestimated is their might
P owers are scary, yet exciting too
E xtreme, even in the later hours
R eally, they can hurt, but on the inside, too
P owers frighten, without being able to enlighten
O ld is new, new is old but my powers stay the same
W ordless, but strong
E lectrokinesis is my superpower
R eal, it truly is
S trong forever

That is my superpower!

Sophia Morath (9)

A Beautiful Night I'll Never Forget

Once upon a magic night,
I lay down, under the mystical sky
Looking up at the silver stars above,
All of a sudden, someone gave me a great big shove.
Before I knew it, we were flying high in the sky,
Two mysterious people passing by,
Twirling into a world of purple and gold
Before my eyes, a beautiful sight to behold.
A world full of beauty and love.
Bright green vines tangled to trees,
Majestic rainbows streaming the sky,
A million colours fill my mind.

India Patel (10)

The Zoo

I really love the zoo,
It's a place for me and you.
The cows were all mooing,
And the chickens were all cooing.
The adults were going, "Whoo!"
And the children were going, "Peekaboo!"
The owl was going *tuwhit-tuwhoo*
And the cat said, "Bring some food."
I went to the car and the car broke down,
And the cat said, "Where's my food?"
I didn't give the cat food, so the cat thought I was rude.

Onyinye Onwuokwu (6)

Home

Out in space, I can't be this lucky...
To be standing here, on the pier of this strange world.
The aliens in the sky point way up high.
Zigzagging five planets, on the farthest one, I lie there in relief.
A ship towards home!

I pass a planet of joy, of war, of love, of fun and then the last...
Towards home!
I turn around to say goodbye, but the aliens had drifted way up high.
Tears swell in my eyes, but everything I need is on my own homeworld!

Erin Murray (8)

My Dragon

What is this celestial beast as bright as the sun who rises in the east?
Her glimmering scales make the stars green with envy,
Her hazel eyes seem never unclean, she soars through the skies,
And tries and tries to face not those who despise,
Her wings they shine as the clocks chime nine.

This beautiful creature not one wrong feature,
And although I know this is a mythical creature,
I wish my dream a fond goodbye, hoping that my dream won't die...

Kanchan Baishkiyar (11)

Performance Of Life

I just want to tell you my dream
Share with you what I want to be.
So, I was walking down the street
With a pounding heart inside of me.
The breeze flew through my hair
And I felt the whole world stare.
I took a step back
And heard somebody say,
"Sing for us today."
A smile spread on my face
And so I started to sing
My voice as sweet as a cupcake.
I felt so alive
As if everything was mine.
It felt like life.

Natalia Kluk (7)

Nightmare

N othing can prepare you for bedtime.
I ntimidating monsters and dragons ready to dine.
G rief floods through you; this is your life's end.
H ollow, there is nothing left. Defend.
T riggers are going off all around you.
M ore shots just miss you, life can't be true.
A nger shoots, your indomitable.
R ight now you wake, dreams are fatal.
E xcited, this will change your life forever...

Hannah Morgan (12)

The Spider Pup

Sometimes, my head is filled with crazy ideas,
And that's why my dreams are mad!
Like when I had the crazy dreams about...
The Spider Pup!

He has,
A cute, little, pink, sock nose
A cool laundry basket hat,
Spotty pants for eyes,
And two black socks for his mouth.

He grows in a minute from the washing on the floor,
Watch out for him in your laundry drawer!

You see, he's not so scary,
Until he turns into a spider and becomes all lairy!

Florence Barlow (8)

The Shadow

As I followed the shadow creeping away,
I thought, *this might be my lucky day.*
Its cloak was swaying in the wind like a dancing tree,
Running after this mysterious figure liked a caged mouse being set free.
Zoom, I was running as fast as a cheetah,
My cheeks felt like a burning heater.

Stop! Stop!

Startled, I woke up in my bed,
Realising that it was just my blanket twisted and twirled all over my head!

Dayna Speker (10)

The Moon Bus

Every night, when I am fast asleep, I dream about moon buses zooming around,
Picking me up, dropping me off, taking me into the unknown.
Buses red and blue, orange and yellow, all of them zooming around in the night.
One by one, they pass me by,
In the dark, star-lit sky.
They dash above the rooves and whizz around the trees,
Hoping not to be seen.
I try to get on one, but then they just disappear,
Perhaps I will just get one next year.

Sophia Magson (10)

Once Upon A Fairy Dream!

Oh, how I wish to be a fairy,
And eating cupcakes and berries,
Flying into the mysterious moonlight,
Eating scrumptious, round lollipops on the way,

In Fairyland, everything flows,
Even pixies with little bows,
Exist in this wonderful magic land!

You can be a tooth fairy,
Flying in the night sky
And grabbing lots of teeth as you pass by,

Oh, how exciting to be a fairy,
You must see this fairyland,
So happy and exciting!

Oishika Das (9)

Weather

The clatter of thunder
The sheet of the rain
Little, tiny ice balls
Poke my windowpane.

Dark, creepy clouds
Thunder, booming, *roar*
Ice splints jaggedly
Knocking at my door.

Gutters overflowing
Sloshing down the walls.
Biting wind is feeling
Howling as it falls.

Safe inside
Warm and as cosy as can be
Proteccted from the weather
And its might and fury.

Mellisa Afram (11)

Wonderville

When I was walking through the streets of Spain,
Asking the rain to give me some brain,
And the next thing I knew,
I was walking through the tracks of Wonderville,
Where Humpty Dumpty was sitting on a tree,
And Henry VIII stepped on a bee,
Peanuts and jelly going into Homer's belly,
As the little critters say,
"White and grey, white and grey, it's May!"
I was filled with happiness once more.

Sabiha Qasimi (9)

Flying Through Space

Flying through space, will I win the race?
Will there be a nursery on Mercury?
Will I find a genius on Venus?
Zooming past stars on my way to Mars,
Will I find life or maybe even a wife?
Will it be quieter on Jupiter?
Will there be a pretty pattern on Saturn?
Will it be poisonous on Uranus?
Will I find my fortune on Neptune?
Is the moon really made of cheese?
Flying through space, will I win the race?

Molly Matthews (10)

Can You Be Your Dreams?

Can you be your dreams?
Unicorns, magical snowflakes
Dracula, dinosaur
Monsters to sun exploding!
Being... thinking... dreaming - aah!
Magical *amazing* mazes.
All about your head! Err,
Nightmares
Come, all will be done by the
I-i-ice monster, evil, *boom!*
Aah!
But I'm tucked in my bed
Was it
A dream?
Can you be my dream?

Tilly Chapman (8)

I Have A Dream

Oh, I have a dream
So beautiful and so sweet
Yes, a lovely dream

Oh, I have a dream
Where we work great as a team
A wonderful dream

Oh, I have a dream
Where we are all treated fair
No matter our hair

Oh, I have a dream
For this world to be so good
So we are all understood

Oh, this is my dream
So beautiful and so sweet
So, this dream I cherish.

Amandeep Bhakar (11)

Bad Dreams

I had a bad dream, I woke at night.
I can't fall asleep, but I'll do what's right.
I'll close my eyes and count to three
And think of a new lovely dream.
I will dream of a magical land,
All creatures, crawling in the sand.
I will find fairies comforting me,
So all the time I'll have good dreams.
I need to wake up and go to eat,
I'll try to forget my horrible dream.

Grace Modesto (8)

A Difference

I've got lots of friends,
And they're all different.
For example,
Poppy likes horses and Emma likes cats.
Aimee likes netball and Isla likes dance!
Freddie like tractors and Jessica likes football.
Payton likes art and Georgia likes Fortnite!
Oh, you're probably wondering,
What do you like, then?
Isn't it obvious what I like?
I like my friends, of course!

Chloe Wilkinson (11)

Falling

Sinking in a sea of black,
Need to find the way out.
All sound is underwater here,
So you cannot shout.
No, you cannot rise,
Don't fight destiny,
By lifting your body up,
You will just lose energy.
Accept that you are stuck,
And cannot escape,
You are one of us now,
So, accept your fate.
Unless you wake up,
From this night-terror,
You are stuck down here,
Yes, you are trapped... *forever!*

Imogen Sims (10)

Dark Shadow Dreams

In the darkness of night
No light.
Scary shadows grow
Feeling like it never will go.

Inside, remember
Outside, remember
You're always safe
Always safe.

Ghosts could scare you
But I'm here beside you.
It's nearly another day

But right now

Today has ended,
Today.
Today.
Today.

All in a dream.

Chloe Clements-Partridge (7)

Famous Adventure

I had a dream that I was an adventurer
It was so much fun to be an adventurer!
Oh, and the best part is Parkour.

Next night, someone came to me and I was surprised
Because the person said, "I'm your fan,"
And then, more people were saying it

And then, I was famous!
I got extremely joyful.
And that was it, my dream.
Happy ending.

Amyra Qoudos (7)

Cornelia

On starlit nights, she glides, her neon wings sparkling in the moonlight.
A dog, bright with wings spread across the horizon, yet she does not bite.
A Collie, not a Poodle,
Her tail thicker than a noodle.
She swoops,
She swirls
And she dives.

Her, she is my dream.
A dog powerful and strong, holding neon wings.
She's beautiful, Cornelia.

Ellen James (8)

Bad Dream

I wake, it strikes 12, I slip out of my bed.
A vivid nightmare whirls around in my head.
Frightened by shadows long and tall,
I tiptoe downstairs, *squeak* goes a ball.
Staring in dismay at a hideous sight,
I gaze at it longer; it gives me a fright.
A shiver down my spine, a bad aching neck,
I find nothing scary, but find I'm in bed.

Frank Crowther (10)

Ice Stars

In my dreams, every night
Every star is shiny, bright
A young girl called Lucy
Sits on her balcony
And admires the stars passing by
High and low
Above the roof,
You can see them from a distant planet.
They travel far into the moonbeam light
And they get colder
Like a big boulder
And frozen stars I can touch.

Eleanor Powlesland (9)

Oh, What A Night!

As it turns dark
I hear a howl or a bark,
As something tiptoes through my dreams,
Something that isn't what it seems.

In my dream,
A wolf is creeping through the night,
Ready to give someone a fright,
And I run, run, run
Then, the dream is done.
I wake up and everything's alright,
Oh, what a night!

Tess Crockford (9)

My Multiverse

Rainbow-coloured stars shine in the sky
So calm, so peaceful, not a peep or a cry
Fluffy animals resting in the sun
Children giggling and having fun
Fairies dancing and prancing around
Soothing choirs making lovely sounds
Calm days basking in rays
Stacks of food that could last for days
But mostly full of amazing memories.

George Hill (9)

Closet

C ruel witches stay in a secret closet to spy,
L ittle nasty creatures that love to lie,
O ver the clothes and into the dark,
S o, that's when the witches' wands start to spark,
E merald green in the cauldron, with smelly rats and their small tails,
T hat is when their plan all comes to a fail.

Teja Vasikauskaite (11)

The Haunted Circus

How did I get here?
As I arrived, I wanted to say goodbye,
I felt my body tingle,
Colours so bright,
I wanted to cry.
As I wiped my eyes, I felt a weird presence beside me,
Their hair was colourful and their face make-up was weird,
He had no beard,
He had funny clothes,
And no toes,
He also had lots of bows.

Anniyah Samoy-Flores (9)

The Amazing Place

When I close my eyes,
I see a world where no one cries,
But there are still challenges you must face,
It is an amazing place,
The sky is as blue as a blue sapphire,
I look to my left and see a house,
Inside the house, I see a mouse,
As I look out of a heart-shaped window,
Behind me is a little, little shadow.

Jessica Woods (9)

Nightmares

Nightmares take over your dreams
Count your fingers to see if they're true
Know that you want to end them
Go away, go away
Go away those nightmares
Dolls and ghouls and venom
Most likely to haunt your body
Nightmares can be found anywhere
Trees, cafés, you name it
They only came for you!

Evan Phillips (8)

Bears

Bears are cuddly and they're cute,
They may look scary but I'll always let them off the hook.
If I ever had one
I'd always give him a bun.
And if I ever lost the bear
I would find it straight away.
So, that's why I love a bear
So, please give it lots of care.

Oliver Ruminas (7)

Disney

I dream of roller coasters,
I dream of Mickey Mouse,
I dream of princesses and what they are all about,
The sun is shining bright in the sky,
And what I dream of next is meeting Minnie Mouse,
I love Disney and the joy it brings
I hope, one day, I will meet these in my dreams.

Sophie Yarranton (8)

I'm Lost

I ran away from it all.
My eyes fixed on a clown who was very tall

Lacking confidence, I knelt down and prayed.
Only my life I had for trade.
Screaming clowns and shiny swords made a Halloween theme.
Then, I wake up, frightened, thinking, *was it all a dream?*

Sophie Grace Kennedy (10)

Unicorns

Unicorns soar
Through the starry night sky.
As the sun rises in the east,
The unicorns land.
Blasts of magic fill the sky.
Fire, air, water, earth and spirit
And as the sky,
Is filled with golden light,
The unicorns canter away.
Away to the wild.

Becky Marshall (9)

One Of My Future Jobs

S inging is what I am very good at.
I t is one of my special/hidden talents.
N othing can stop me from singing.
G ood, it is very good for me to sing.
E ager, I am very eager to become a singer.
R eady, I am ready to be a singer!

Kiana Gour (10)

Seaside Poem

The soft, yellow sand, I walk across it,
I see the calm blue sea,
I step in with my surfboard and paddle away,
The sea is cold like the Arctic Ocean,
I jump into the cold water and swim away to Africa and France,
But I met some mermaids,
And as we play,
It feels like heaven...

Rae Denton (6)

Once Upon A Dream

Once, I dreamt of a fairy who came to my house, she saw a little mouse.
Upon sight of the mouse, she let out a scream.
An astonished mouse screamed back as they both burst into laughter.
Dream big, bold and bright.

Rose Field (7)

Lesson Of Life

Don't drive faster than a guardian
Angel can fly

Don't say you're my
Friend when you
Plan on saying
Goodbye

Don't be ashamed
Of anything you do

'Cause you have me and I
Have you.

Aaisha Munshi (10)

To Dream...

D reams are a wonderful, peaceful experience.
R unning free, you can just relax and
E njoy it. Just close your eyes and imagine.
A nything can happen to those who drift off to the
M agical paradise of dreams...

Thomas Living (11)

The Whale Tale

The pale whale ate a stale snail
He started to ail
His tail started to flail
Well, he tried but he failed
The whale started to sail
But got sent to jail
For eating the snail
What a whale of a tale!

Nico Kitson (7)

I Dream To Have A Golden Retriever

I dream to have a Golden Retriever
That is very soft and fluffy.
I want a small Golden Retriever puppy;
A Golden Retriever that shines like gold.

Còiseam Young (8)

YoungWriters® Est. 1991

YOUNG WRITERS INFORMATION

We hope you have enjoyed reading this book – and that you will continue to in the coming years.

If you're a young writer who enjoys reading and creative writing, or the parent of an enthusiastic poet or story writer, do visit our website **www.youngwriters.co.uk**. Here you will find free competitions, workshops and games, as well as recommended reads, a poetry glossary and our blog.

If you would like to order further copies of this book, or any of our other titles, then please give us a call or visit **www.youngwriters.co.uk**.

Young Writers
Remus House
Coltsfoot Drive
Peterborough
PE2 9BF
(01733) 890066
info@youngwriters.co.uk

YoungWritersUK   **YoungWritersCW**
youngwriterscw   **youngwriterscw**